MathFlare

Name: __________________________

Class: __________

Teacher: __________________________

Introduction

As parents and educators, we recognize the pivotal role mathematics plays in shaping a child's academic journey and future success. Yet, the path to mathematical proficiency can often seem daunting, fraught with challenges and complexities. That's where the transformative power of MathFlare Workbooks shine through, illuminating the way forward with clarity, precision, and purpose.

Introducing MathFlare Workbooks – a beacon of guidance, a testament to excellence, and a catalyst for achievement. Crafted with meticulous care and expertise, MathFlare Workbooks stand as paragons of educational excellence, designed to nurture young minds, ignite a passion for learning, and develop a deep-rooted understanding of mathematical concepts.

Picture this: your child eagerly delves into the pages of Mathflare Workbook, greeted by a step-by-step guide illuminated with vivid examples that demystify complex mathematical concepts. With each turn of the page, they embark on a journey of discovery, encountering thoughtfully curated practice questions that reinforce learning and hone problem-solving skills. And when they unveil the answers to those very questions, a sense of accomplishment blossoms within them – a tangible reward for their hard work and dedication.

But MathFlare Workbooks are more than just tools for learning; they are pathways to comprehension, fostering a deep-seated understanding of mathematical concepts through a sequential, logical flow. From fundamental principles to advanced problem-solving strategies, every chapter builds upon the last, ensuring a robust foundation upon which future knowledge can be constructed.

As parents, we yearn for nothing more than to see our children thrive, to witness the spark of inspiration ignited within them as they conquer academic challenges with confidence and poise. MathFlare Workbooks serve as partners in this noble endeavor, offering not just practice questions, but the keys to unlocking a world of opportunity.

And for teachers, MathFlare Workbooks stand as invaluable allies in the quest to cultivate mathematical proficiency in the classroom. With answers readily available, instructors can focus on guiding and nurturing their students, confident in the knowledge that MathFlare Workbooks provide a solid framework upon which to build.

In the pages of MathFlare Workbooks, we find not just the promise of academic excellence, but the seeds of a brighter tomorrow. So let us embrace the power of mathematics, let us champion the journey of learning, and let us pave the way for a generation of young minds poised to shape the world. With MathFlare Workbooks as our guide, the possibilities are infinite, and the future, bright.

Table of Contents

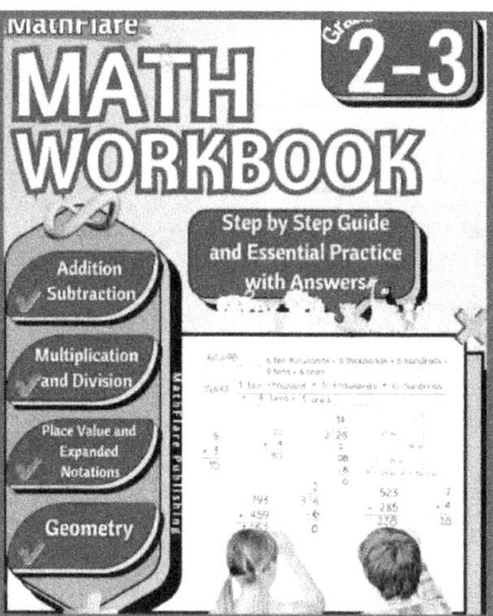

MathFlare
MATH WORKBOOK
Grade 5
Step by Step Guide and Essential Practice with Answers
Multiplication Division
Place Value and Expanded Notations
Fractions and Geometry
Unit Conversion
MathFlare Publishing

MathFlare
MATH WORKBOOK
Grade 5-6
Step by Step Guide and Essential Practice with Answers
Multiplication Division
Place Value and Expanded Notations
Fractions and Geometry
Units and Statistics
MathFlare Publishing

MathFlare
MATH WORKBOOK
Grade 6
Step by Step Guide and Essential Practice with Answers
Integers and Statistics
Arithmetic and Pre-Algebra
Fractions and Geometry
Ratio and Percentage
MathFlare Publishing

MathFlare
MATH WORKBOOK
Grade 6-7
Step by Step Guide and Essential Practice with Answers
Arithmetic and Pre-Algebra
Ratio, Percent Proportion
Geometry
Statistics
MathFlare Publishing

MathFlare
MATH WORKBOOK
Grade 7
Step by Step Guide and Essential Practice with Answers
Pre-Algebra
Ratio, Percent Proportion
Geometry
Statistics
MathFlare Publishing

MathFlare
MATH WORKBOOK
Grade 7-8
Step by Step Guide and Essential Practice with Answers
Pre-Algebra
Ratio, Percent Proportion
Geometry and Cartesian Plane
Statistics
MathFlare Publishing

MathFlare
MATH WORKBOOK
Grade 8-9
Step by Step Guide and Essential Practice with Answers
Pre-Algebra
Ratio, Proportion and Percentage
Linear Equations
Geometry and Cartesian Plane
MathFlare Publishing

MathFlare
MATH WORKBOOK
Grade 8
Step by Step Guide and Essential Practice with Answers
Pre-Algebra
Percentage
Linear Equations
Geometry
MathFlare Publishing

Place Value and Expanded Notations

Place value tells us the value of a digit in a number based on where it's placed.

Imagine we have the number 45,643. It has five digits: 4, 5, 6, 4, and 3.

Now, each digit holds a special place. Let's break down the number 45,643:

- The first digit, 4, is in the ten thousands place.

- The second digit, 5, is in the thousands place.

- The third digit, 6, is in the hundreds place.

- The fourth digit, 4, is in the tens place.

- The fifth digit, 3, is in the ones place.

When we add these values together, we find the value of the entire number:

$$40000 + 5000 + 600 + 40 + 3 = 45,643$$

Expanded notation helps us see the individual value of each digit in a number and how they contribute to the overall value of the number. It's like breaking down a big puzzle into smaller pieces to understand it better!

So, in expanded notation, we can write 45,643 as: 40000 (from ten thousand place) + 5000 (from thousands place) + 600 (from the hundreds place) + 40 (from the tens place) + 3 (from the ones place).

Let's solve some problems:

Place value of the underlined digit:

$$1\underline{3}.027 = \underline{\quad 3 \text{ ones} \quad}$$

Expanded notations:

$\underline{\quad 7{,}409.3 \quad}$ 7 thousands + 4 hundreds + 9 ones + 3 tenths

52,374   5 ten thousands + 2 thousands + 3 hundreds + 7 tens + 4 ones

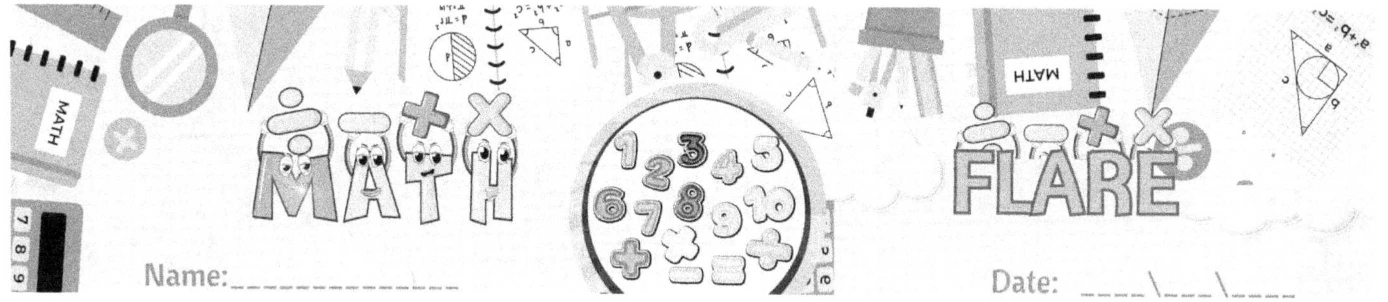

Place Value

Determine the place value of the underlined digit.

1. 7,79<u>2</u> = _______________

2. 5,6<u>6</u>7 = _______________

3. 9,59<u>1</u> = _______________

4. 2,55<u>9</u> = _______________

5. <u>6</u>,805 = _______________

6. 8,80<u>6</u> = _______________

7. 22<u>7</u> = _______________

8. <u>7</u>,648 = _______________

9. 4,39<u>3</u> = _______________

10. <u>4</u>,841 = _______________

11. <u>4</u>,745 = _______________

12. <u>7</u>,441 = _______________

13. 4,<u>7</u>76 = _______________

14. 5,33<u>4</u> = _______________

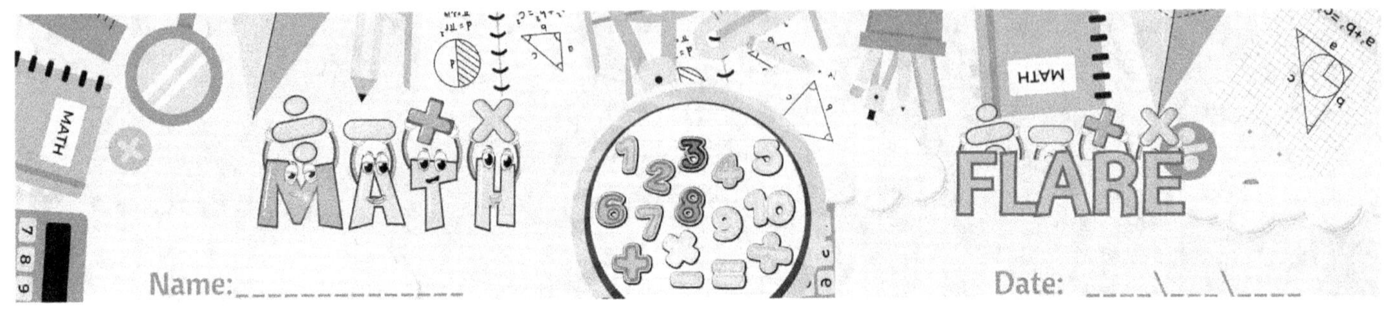

15. 5,<u>2</u>00 = _______________

16. 5,18<u>4</u> = _______________

17. <u>2</u>,916 = _______________

18. <u>8</u>,018 = _______________

19. <u>7</u>,314 = _______________

20. 4,<u>1</u>73 = _______________

21. 1,<u>9</u>37 = _______________

22. <u>2</u>,706 = _______________

23. 2,7<u>0</u>5 = _______________

24. <u>3</u>,384 = _______________

25. 8,<u>8</u>50 = _______________

26. 7,50<u>7</u> = _______________

27. <u>5</u>,868 = _______________

28. 2,0<u>0</u>9 = _______________

29. 3,<u>5</u>37 = _______________

30. <u>8</u>98 = _______________

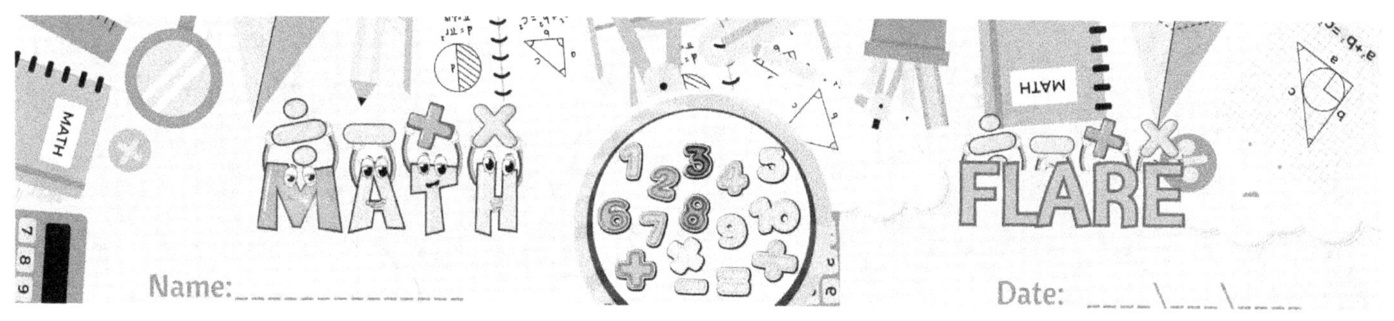

31. 6,342 = _______________

32. 5,825 = _______________

33. 2,031 = _______________

34. 3,007 = _______________

35. 2,965 = _______________

36. 9,463 = _______________

37. 4,337 = _______________

38. 2,441 = _______________

39. 9,931 = _______________

40. 2,789 = _______________

41. 5,270 = _______________

42. 2,160 = _______________

43. 1,696 = _______________

44. 8,533 = _______________

45. 2,841 = _______________

46. 4,310 = _______________

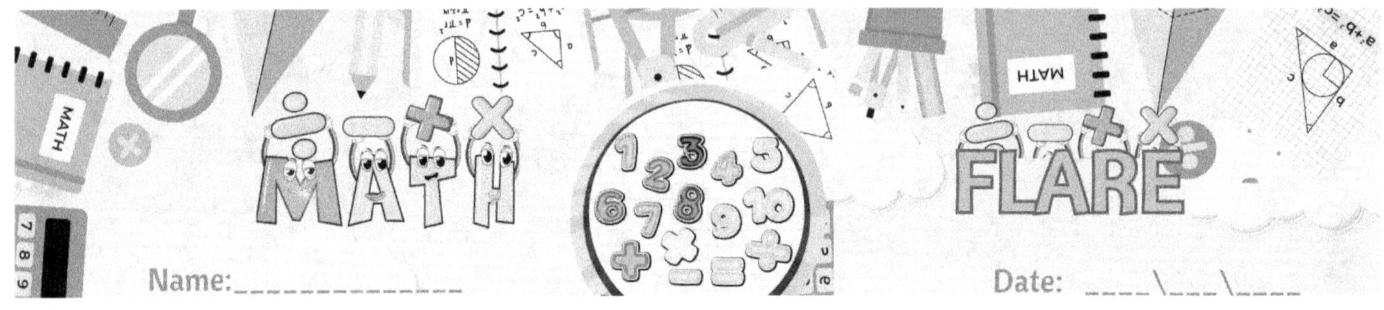

47. 8,9_5_1 = ___________________

48. 3,73_8_ = ___________________

49. 3,8_5_8 = ___________________

50. 3,6_6_8 = ___________________

51. 3,_2_89 = ___________________

52. 9,8_04_ = ___________________

53. 4,82_0_ = ___________________

54. _8_,958 = ___________________

55. _2_,755 = ___________________

56. 5,_0_87 = ___________________

57. 2,_9_62 = ___________________

58. 6,20_7_ = ___________________

59. _3_,708 = ___________________

60. _9_,297 = ___________________

61. 2,_9_39 = ___________________

62. 8,21_7_ = ___________________

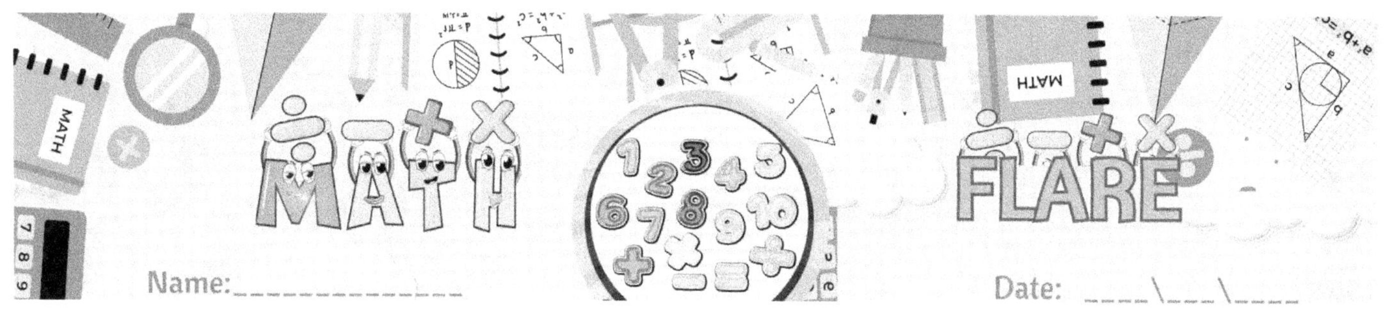

63. 4,11<u>2</u> = _______________

64. <u>3</u>,495 = _______________

65. <u>8</u>,498 = _______________

66. 8,9<u>1</u>9 = _______________

67. <u>5</u>,411 = _______________

68. 1,7<u>7</u>0 = _______________

69. 2,3<u>7</u>0 = _______________

70. 5,73<u>6</u> = _______________

71. 8<u>4</u>8 = _______________

72. <u>4</u>76 = _______________

73. <u>8</u>,085 = _______________

74. <u>4</u>,526 = _______________

75. 8,9<u>0</u>2 = _______________

76. 9,<u>7</u>75 = _______________

77. 1,<u>0</u>11 = _______________

78. 4,1<u>7</u>2 = _______________

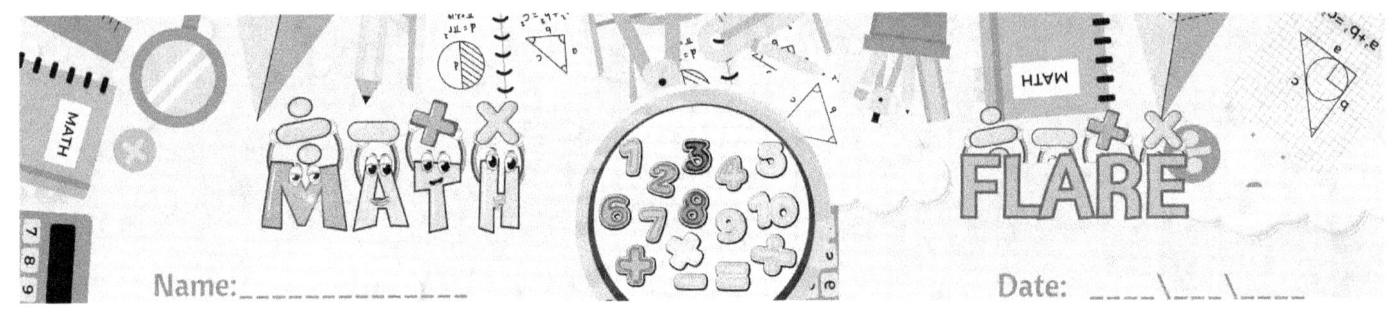

79. 5̲44 = _________________

80. 4,5̲42 = _________________

81. 8̲,555 = _________________

82. 2,131̲ = _________________

83. 8,1̲50 = _________________

84. 9̲,868 = _________________

85. 7,60̲8 = _________________

86. 6̲,537 = _________________

87. 1,0̲06 = _________________

88. 3,0̲72 = _________________

89. 25̲3 = _________________

90. 7,87̲7 = _________________

91. 6̲,502 = _________________

92. 8,12̲8 = _________________

93. 8,73̲2 = _________________

94. 63̲5 = _________________

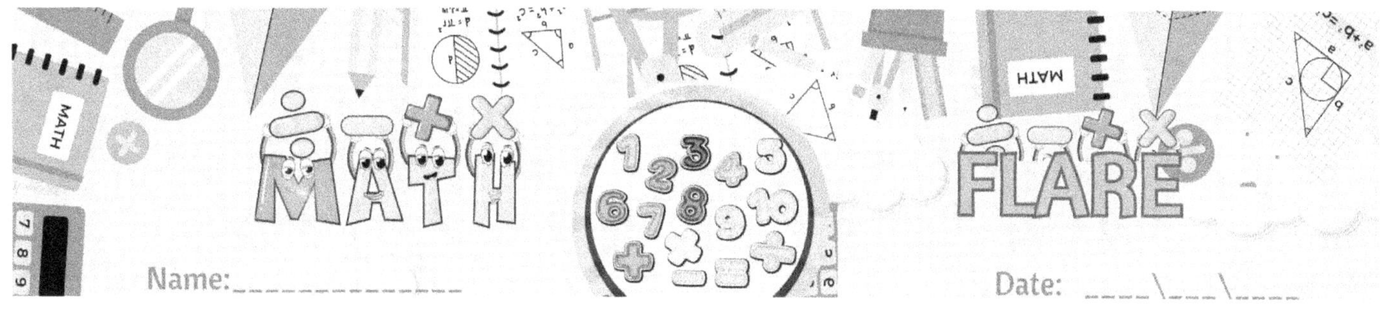

Name:_______________   Date: _________________

Place Value: Expanded Notation

Provide the expanded notation for each value.

95. ________________ 9 thousands + 3 hundreds + 6 tens + 5 ones

96. ________________ 6 thousands + 6 tens + 7 ones

97. ________________ 3 thousands + 6 hundreds + 3 tens + 1 one

98. ________________ 7 thousands + 7 hundreds + 6 tens + 2 ones

99. ________________ 2 thousands + 1 hundred + 4 tens + 3 ones

100. ________________ 3 thousands + 4 hundreds + 4 tens + 6 ones

101. ________________ 4 thousands + 8 hundreds + 7 tens + 2 ones

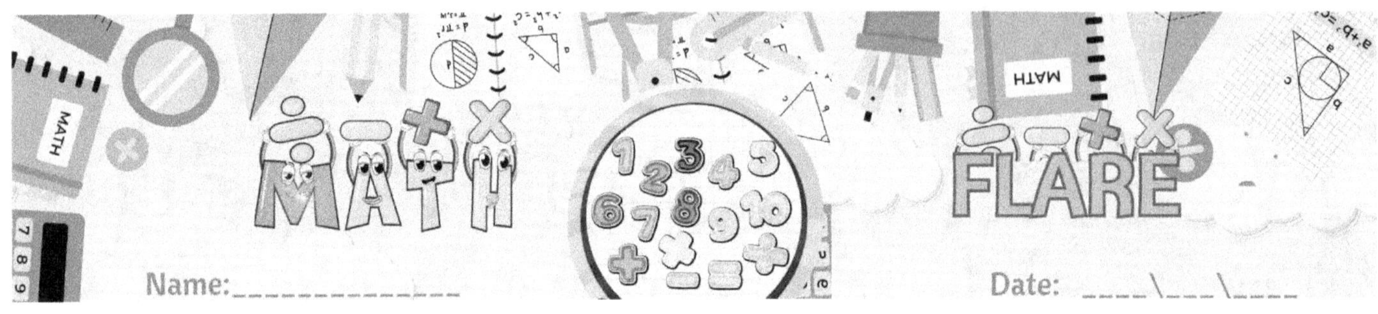

102. ________________ 5 thousands + 9 hundreds + 6 tens + 2 ones

103. ________________ 4 thousands + 4 hundreds + 2 tens + 6 ones

104. ________________ 7 thousands + 1 hundred + 7 tens

105. ________________ 6 thousands + 4 hundreds + 9 tens

106. ________________ 9 thousands + 6 hundreds + 2 ones

107. ________________ 6 thousands + 6 hundreds + 4 tens

108. ________________ 3 thousands + 7 hundreds + 2 tens + 2 ones

109. ________________ 2 thousands + 7 hundreds + 6 tens + 3 ones

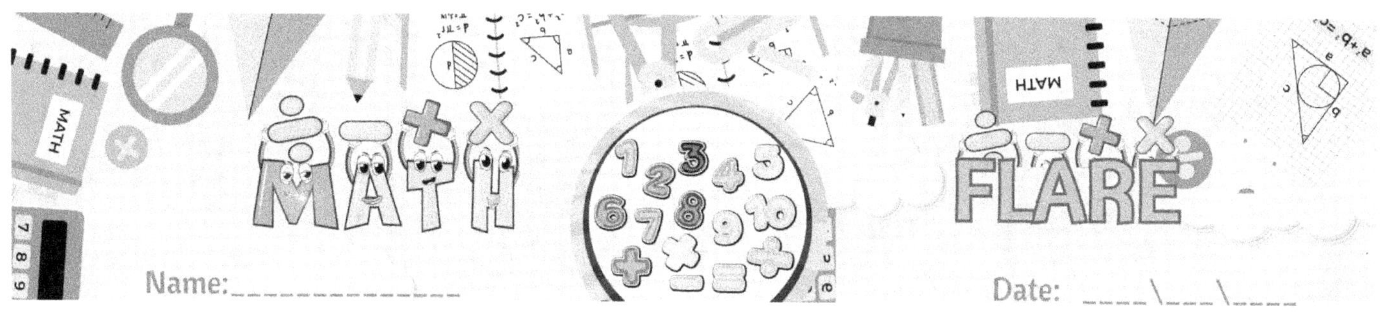

110. _______________ 3 hundreds + 7 tens + 3 ones

111. _______________ 7 thousands + 3 hundreds + 5 tens + 5 ones

112. _______________ 9 thousands + 7 hundreds + 6 tens + 9 ones

113. _______________ 6 tens + 6 ones

114. _______________ 4 thousands + 7 hundreds + 1 ten + 7 ones

115. _______________ 3 thousands + 3 hundreds + 6 tens + 6 ones

116. _______________ 5 hundreds + 8 tens

117. _______________ 6 thousands + 2 hundreds + 2 tens

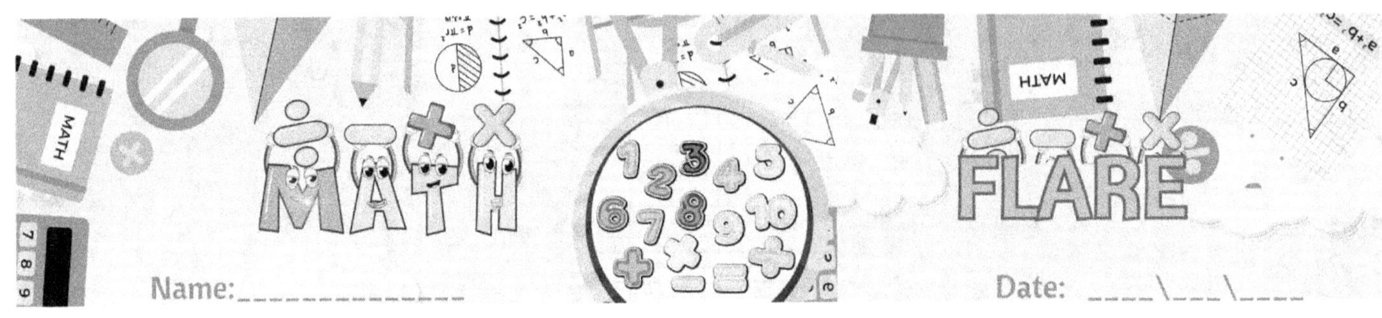

Name:_________________   Date: _____________

118. ________________ 5 thousands + 5 hundreds + 6 ones

119. ________________ 9 thousands + 7 hundreds + 5 tens + 3 ones

120. ________________ 9 thousands + 5 hundreds + 5 tens + 8 ones

121. ________________ 4 thousands + 4 hundreds + 2 tens + 9 ones

122. ________________ 6 thousands + 3 hundreds + 4 tens + 7 ones

123. ________________ 2 thousands + 3 hundreds + 1 ten

124. ________________ 8 thousands + 5 hundreds + 2 tens + 6 ones

125. ________________ 9 thousands + 2 hundreds + 6 tens + 7 ones

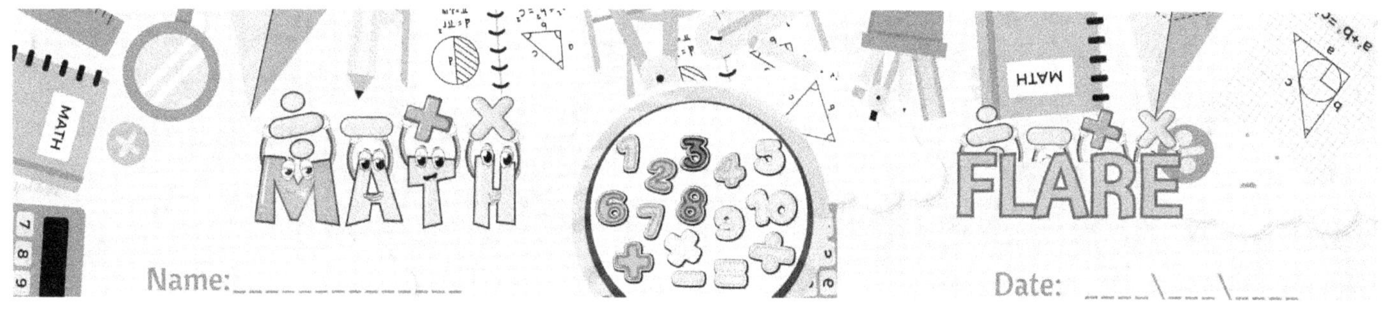

126. ___________ 7 thousands + 4 hundreds + 7 tens

127. ___________ 3 thousands + 2 hundreds + 9 tens + 7 ones

128. ___________ 7 thousands + 1 hundred + 8 tens + 6 ones

129. ___________ 9 thousands + 6 hundreds + 8 tens + 9 ones

130. ___________ 7 thousands + 3 hundreds + 8 tens + 6 ones

131. ___________ 4 thousands + 1 hundred + 8 ones

132. ___________ 2 thousands + 8 hundreds + 8 tens + 8 ones

133. ___________ 4 thousands + 2 tens + 9 ones

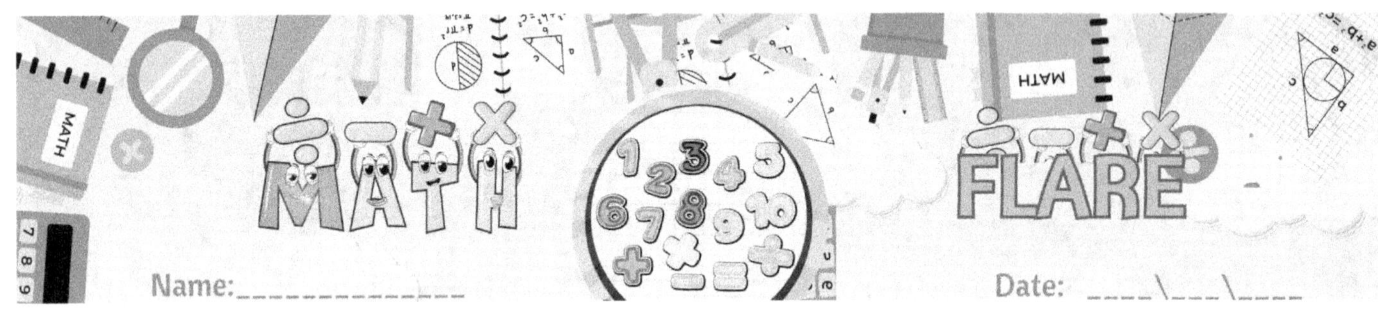

134. _____________ 8 hundreds + 2 tens + 9 ones

135. _____________ 6 thousands + 9 hundreds + 1 ten + 2 ones

136. _____________ 5 thousands + 7 hundreds + 8 tens + 1 one

137. _____________ 4 thousands + 1 hundred + 9 tens + 5 ones

138. _____________ 2 thousands + 9 hundreds + 4 tens + 9 ones

139. _____________ 6 thousands + 2 hundreds + 3 tens + 7 ones

140. _____________ 3 thousands + 8 hundreds + 9 tens + 9 ones

141. _____________ 9 thousands + 9 hundreds + 2 tens + 8 ones

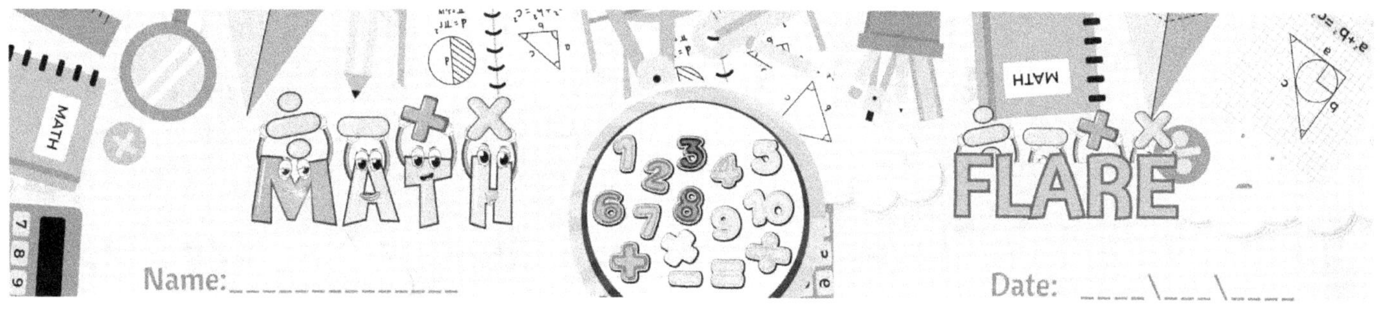

142. _______________ 1 thousand + 8 hundreds + 8 tens + 1 one

143. _______________ 2 thousands + 4 hundreds + 9 tens + 5 ones

144. _______________ 8 thousands + 6 hundreds + 3 tens + 3 ones

145. _______________ 4 thousands + 7 hundreds + 5 tens + 4 ones

146. _______________ 1 thousand + 5 hundreds + 6 tens + 1 one

147. _______________ 8 thousands + 8 hundreds + 3 tens + 9 ones

148. _______________ 4 thousands + 7 hundreds + 6 tens + 5 ones

149. _______________ 5 thousands + 2 hundreds + 3 tens + 7 ones

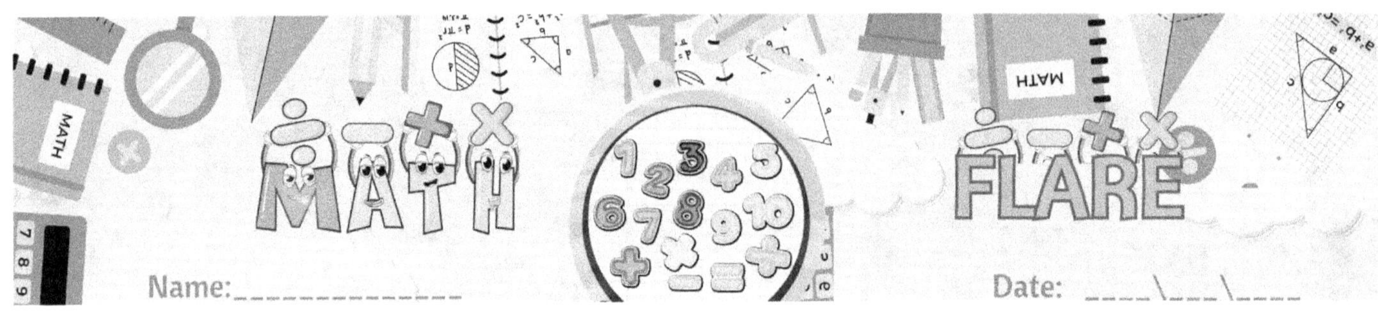

150. _________________ 8 thousands + 7 hundreds + 8 tens + 5 ones

151. _________________ 9 thousands + 8 hundreds + 4 tens + 6 ones

152. _________________ 8 thousands + 1 hundred + 2 tens + 4 ones

153. _________________ 8 thousands + 8 ones

154. _________________ 2 thousands + 5 hundreds + 8 tens + 4 ones

155. _________________ 9 thousands + 1 ten + 6 ones

156. _________________ 8 thousands + 5 hundreds + 2 tens + 3 ones

157. _________________ 3 thousands + 6 hundreds + 5 tens + 3 ones

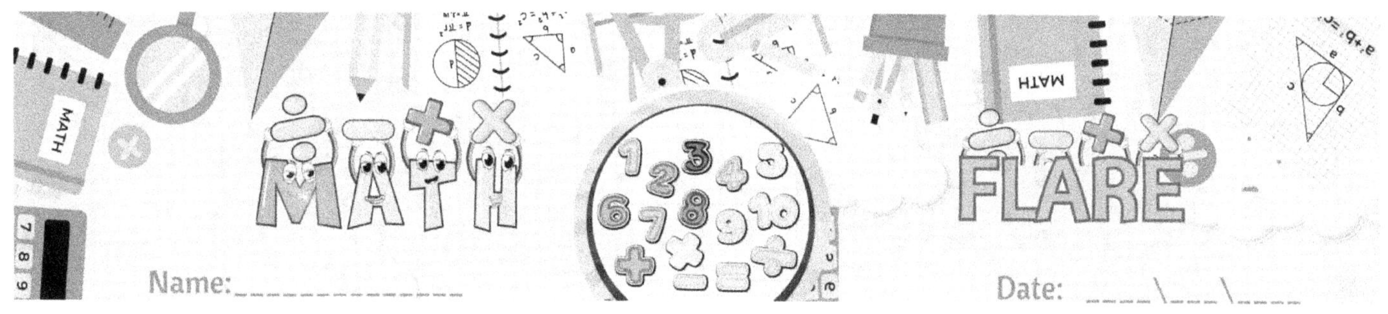

158. ___________ 5 thousands + 8 hundreds + 9 tens + 8 ones

159. ___________ 7 thousands + 9 hundreds + 1 one

160. ___________ 9 thousands + 1 ten + 8 ones

161. ___________ 6 thousands + 3 hundreds + 5 ones

162. ___________ 9 thousands + 4 hundreds + 5 tens + 3 ones

163. ___________ 4 thousands + 3 tens + 1 one

164. ___________ 5 thousands + 3 hundreds + 7 tens + 6 ones

165. ___________ 6 thousands + 2 hundreds + 6 tens + 4 ones

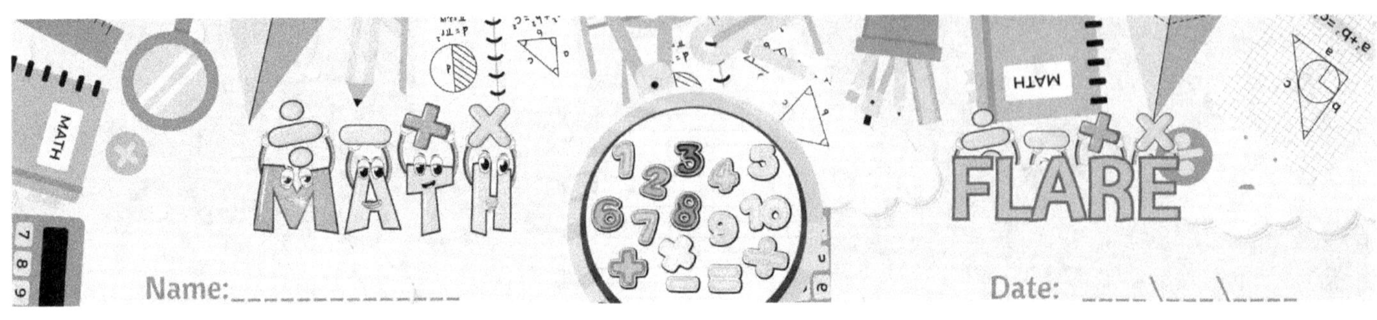

Name:________________   Date: ___________

166. ______________   4 thousands + 4 hundreds + 6 tens + 7 ones

167. ______________   5 thousands + 7 hundreds + 4 tens + 1 one

168. ______________   9 thousands + 2 hundreds + 3 tens + 6 ones

169. ______________   7 thousands + 8 hundreds + 5 ones

170. ______________   7 thousands + 5 hundreds + 8 tens + 4 ones

171. ______________   6 thousands + 3 hundreds + 8 tens + 4 ones

172. ______________   3 thousands + 2 hundreds + 7 tens + 2 ones

173. ______________   9 thousands + 2 hundreds + 6 tens + 8 ones

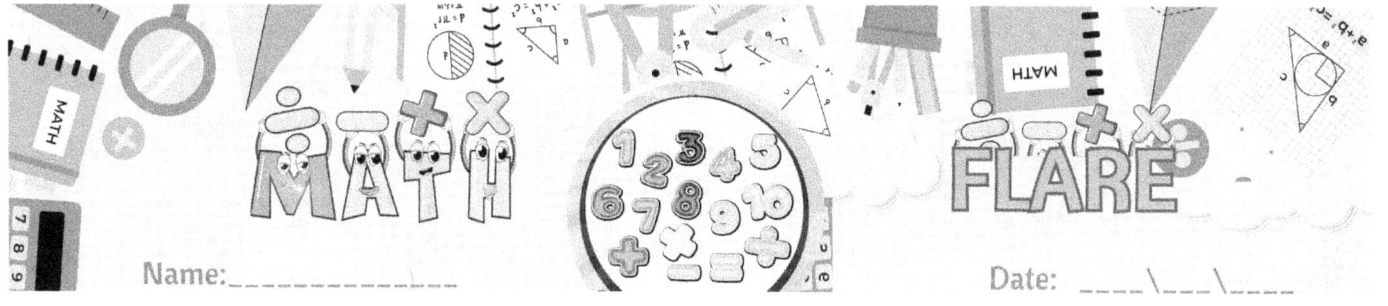

Place Value: Expanded Notation

Provide the expanded notation for each value.

174. 9,918 ___________________

175. 9,824 ___________________

176. 4,384 ___________________

177. 6,824 ___________________

178. 9,749 ___________________

179. 4,822 ___________________

180. 6,426 ___________________

181. 9,877 ___________________

182. 5,040 ________________________

183. 281 ________________________

184. 8,946 ________________________

185. 4,647 ________________________

186. 6,753 ________________________

187. 2,191 ________________________

188. 3,207 ________________________

189. 1,793 ________________________

190. 7,634 ________________________

191. 8,739 ________________________

192. 3,391 ______________________

193. 7,084 ______________________

194. 1,785 ______________________

195. 5,296 ______________________

196. 4,025 ______________________

197. 1,681 ______________________

198. 8,607 ______________________

199. 964 ______________________

200. 1,454 ______________________

201. 8,649 ______________________

202. 9,663 __________________

203. 8,153 __________________

204. 6,106 __________________

205. 5,818 __________________

206. 4,610 __________________

207. 1,593 __________________

208. 1,923 __________________

209. 9,067 __________________

210. 8,013 __________________

211. 8,154 __________________

212. 1,834 _______________________

213. 626 _______________________

214. 1,185 _______________________

215. 1,913 _______________________

216. 5,445 _______________________

217. 9,174 _______________________

218. 6,905 _______________________

219. 3,293 _______________________

220. 7,754 _______________________

221. 9,976 _______________________

222. 7,902 _________________

223. 8,642 _________________

224. 6,623 _________________

225. 4,090 _________________

226. 4,631 _________________

227. 6,720 _________________

228. 4,623 _________________

229. 5,800 _________________

230. 2,704 _________________

231. 8,215 _________________

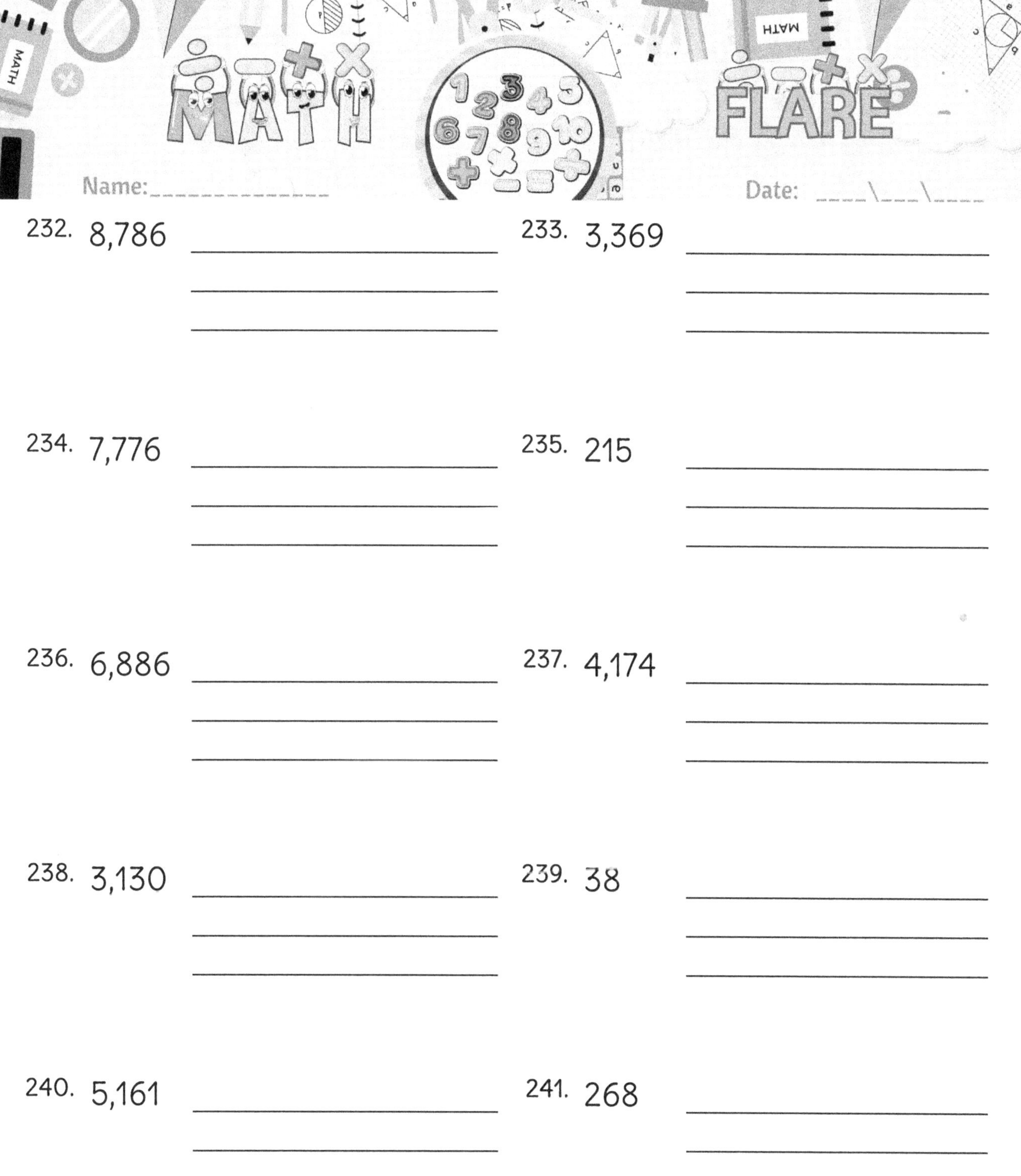

232. 8,786 _______________________

233. 3,369 _______________________

234. 7,776 _______________________

235. 215 _______________________

236. 6,886 _______________________

237. 4,174 _______________________

238. 3,130 _______________________

239. 38 _______________________

240. 5,161 _______________________

241. 268 _______________________

242. 4,140 _______________

243. 3,779 _______________

244. 9,479 _______________

245. 6,906 _______________

246. 2,766 _______________

247. 5,900 _______________

248. 9,871 _______________

249. 9,850 _______________

250. 4,850 _______________

251. 4,775 _______________

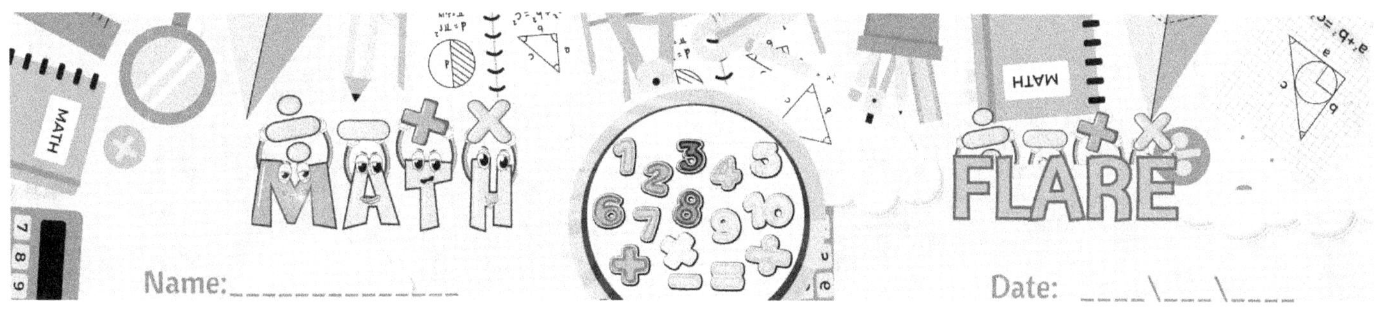

Place Value: Expanded Notation

Provide the expanded notation for each value.

252. ____________ 6,000 + 600 + 80 + 1

253. ____________ 3,000 + 900 + 10 + 6

254. ____________ 3,000 + 2

255. ____________ 6,000 + 500 + 20 + 7

256. ____________ 1,000 + 200 + 7

257. ____________ 1,000 + 900 + 70 + 4

258. ____________ 4,000 + 600 + 60 + 9

259. ____________ 6,000 + 500 + 50 + 2

260. ____________ 9,000 + 900 + 20 + 6

261. ____________ 3,000 + 400 + 50 + 4

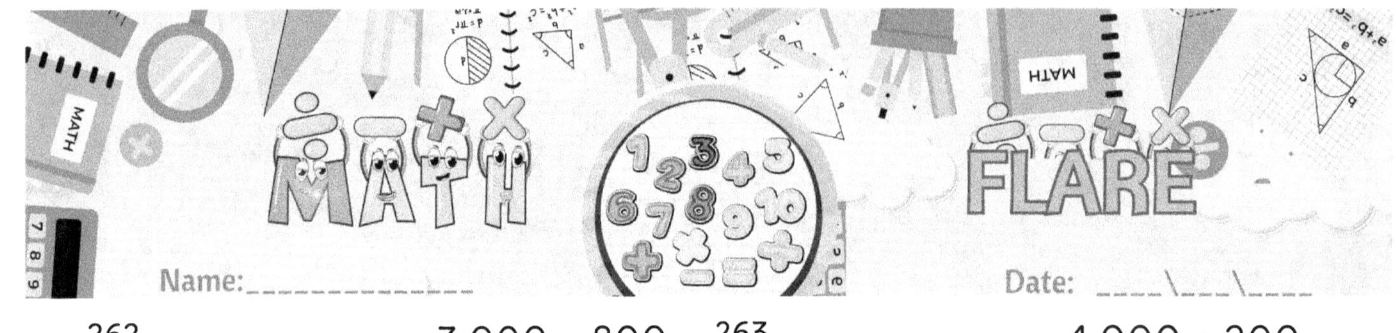

262. ________________   3,000 + 800 + 50 + 3

263. ________________   4,000 + 200 + 50 + 1

264. ________________   7,000 + 600 + 10 + 1

265. ________________   3,000 + 200 + 80

266. ________________   6,000 + 100 + 70 + 5

267. ________________   900 + 70 + 2

268. ________________   6,000 + 800 + 6

269. ________________   500 + 70 + 7

270. ________________   2,000 + 500 + 60 + 2

271. ________________   8,000 + 70 + 1

272. ________________   5,000 + 100 + 60 + 2

273. ________________   1,000 + 50 + 7

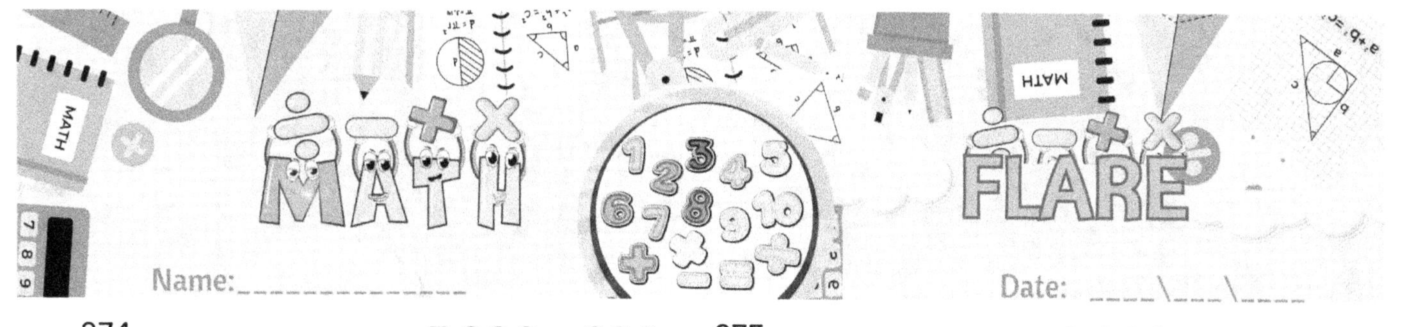

274. ______________ 7,000 + 800 + 20 + 5

275. ______________ 2,000 + 100 + 30 + 3

276. ______________ 1,000 + 800 + 50 + 9

277. ______________ 8,000 + 300 + 20 + 3

278. ______________ 2,000 + 100 + 80 + 5

279. ______________ 4,000 + 800 + 40 + 6

280. ______________ 800 + 30 + 8

281. ______________ 1,000 + 500 + 80 + 5

282. ______________ 4,000 + 300 + 50 + 3

283. ______________ 4,000 + 800 + 40 + 1

284. ______________ 2,000 + 400 + 10 + 8

285. ______________ 7,000 + 900 + 60 + 1

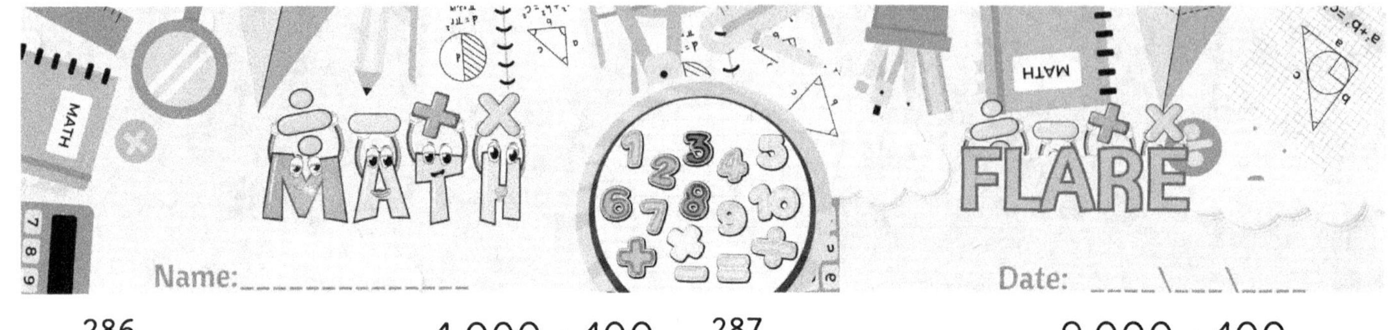

Name:______________   Date: ______________

286. __________ 4,000 + 100 + 40 + 2

287. __________ 9,000 + 100

288. __________ 1,000 + 400 + 50 + 8

289. __________ 6,000 + 100 + 30 + 2

290. __________ 1,000 + 600 + 30 + 3

291. __________ 3,000 + 500 + 10 + 2

292. __________ 7,000 + 200 + 30 + 5

293. __________ 1,000 + 100 + 80 + 4

294. __________ 2,000 + 800 + 20 + 4

295. __________ 3,000 + 300 + 80 + 3

296. __________ 6,000 + 200 + 40 + 6

297. __________ 4,000 + 300 + 70 + 3

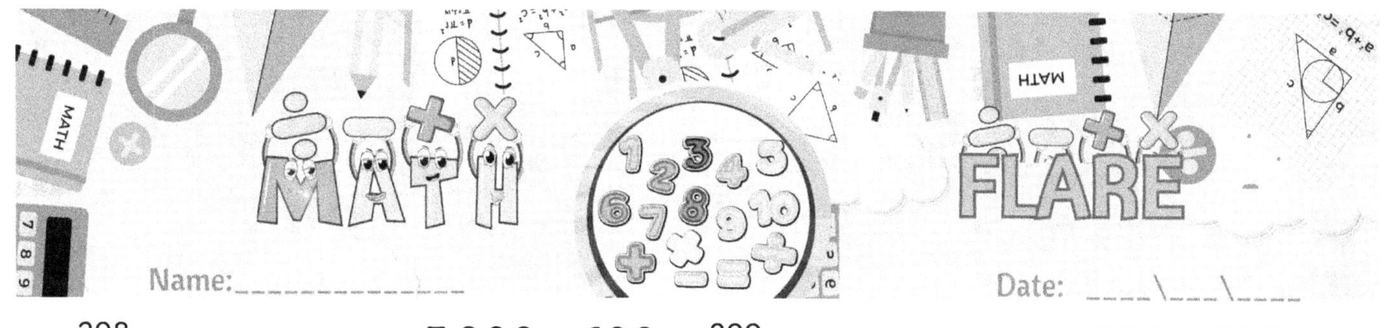

298. _____________   7,000 + 600 + 90 + 6

299. _____________   8,000 + 700 + 4

300. _____________   7,000 + 300 + 6

301. _____________   5,000 + 80 + 8

302. _____________   7,000 + 100 + 70 + 9

303. _____________   4,000 + 200 + 80 + 8

304. _____________   8,000 + 100 + 80

305. _____________   2,000 + 100 + 90 + 7

306. _____________   1,000 + 10 + 4

307. _____________   5,000 + 600 + 20 + 5

308. _____________   6,000 + 90

309. _____________   800 + 70

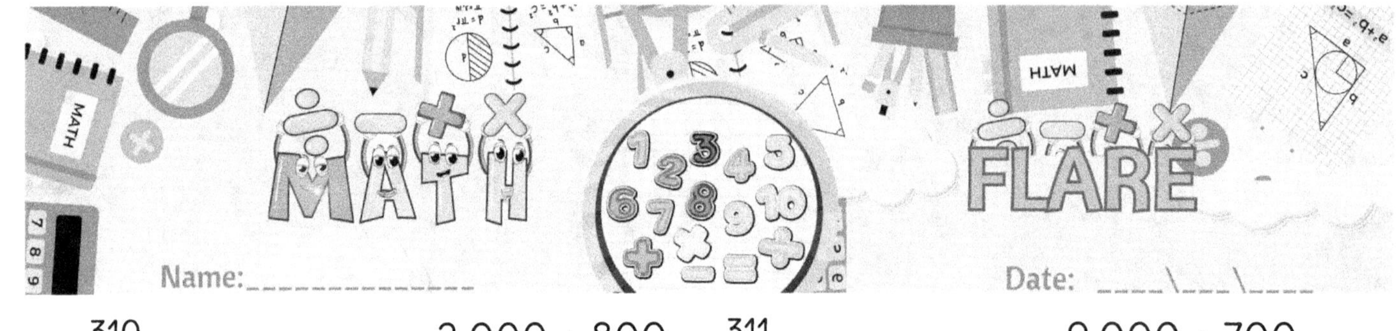

310. _______________   2,000 + 800 + 80 + 3

311. _______________   9,000 + 700 + 80 + 7

312. _______________   9,000 + 800 + 20 + 2

313. _______________   5,000 + 700 + 10 + 5

314. _______________   8,000 + 300 + 40 + 2

315. _______________   9,000 + 100 + 1

316. _______________   9,000 + 10 + 1

317. _______________   1,000 + 800 + 30 + 4

318. _______________   9,000 + 600 + 50

319. _______________   9,000 + 100 + 30 + 7

320. _______________   7,000 + 70 + 4

321. _______________   9,000 + 500 + 10 + 3

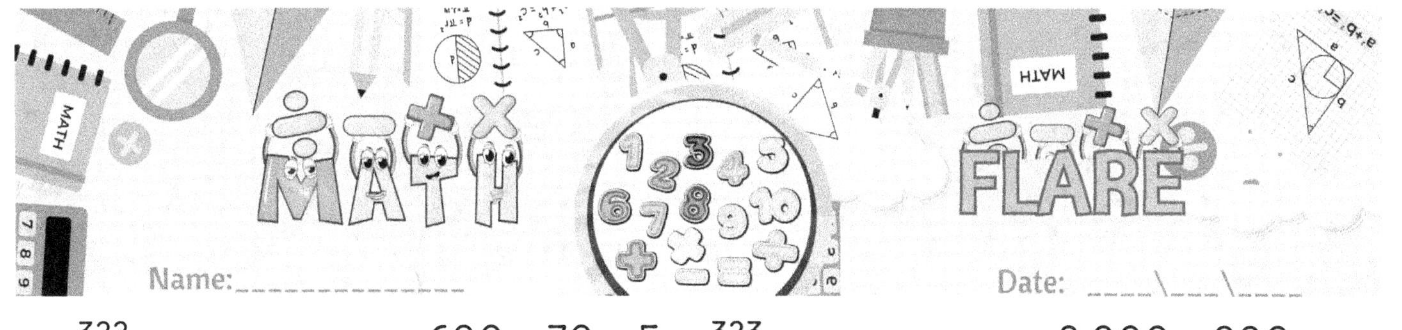

322. __________ $600 + 70 + 5$

323. __________ $8,000 + 900 + 40 + 3$

324. __________ $9,000 + 40 + 9$

325. __________ $3,000 + 900 + 70 + 9$

326. __________ $8,000 + 200 + 30 + 3$

327. __________ $4,000 + 400 + 40 + 4$

328. __________ $5,000 + 800 + 80 + 6$

329. __________ $7,000 + 400 + 80 + 5$

330. __________ $600 + 20 + 8$

331. __________ $3,000 + 400 + 80 + 1$

332. __________ $7,000 + 500 + 30 + 9$

333. __________ $5,000 + 700 + 40 + 9$

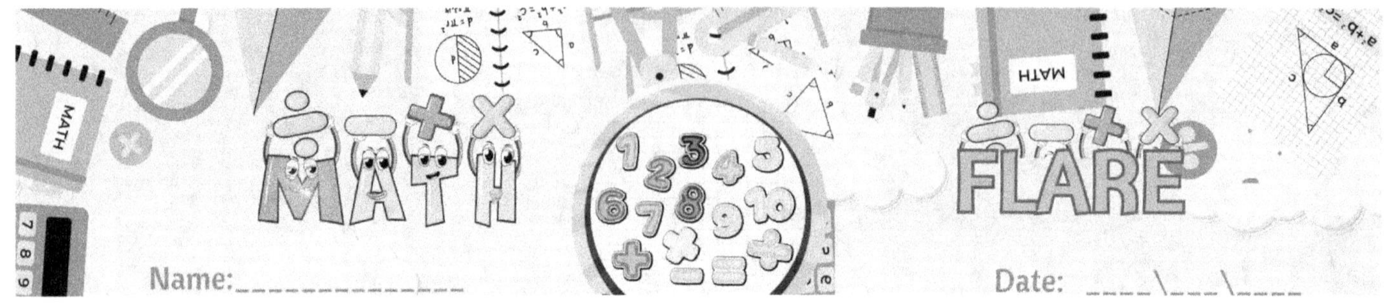

Place Value: Expanded Notation

Provide the expanded notation for each value.

334. 4,405 ___________________

335. 65 ___________________

336. 6,661 ___________________

337. 222 ___________________

338. 6,948 ___________________

339. 8,516 ___________________

340. 3,011 ___________________

341. 589 ___________________

342. 1,463 ___________________

343. 8,749 ___________________

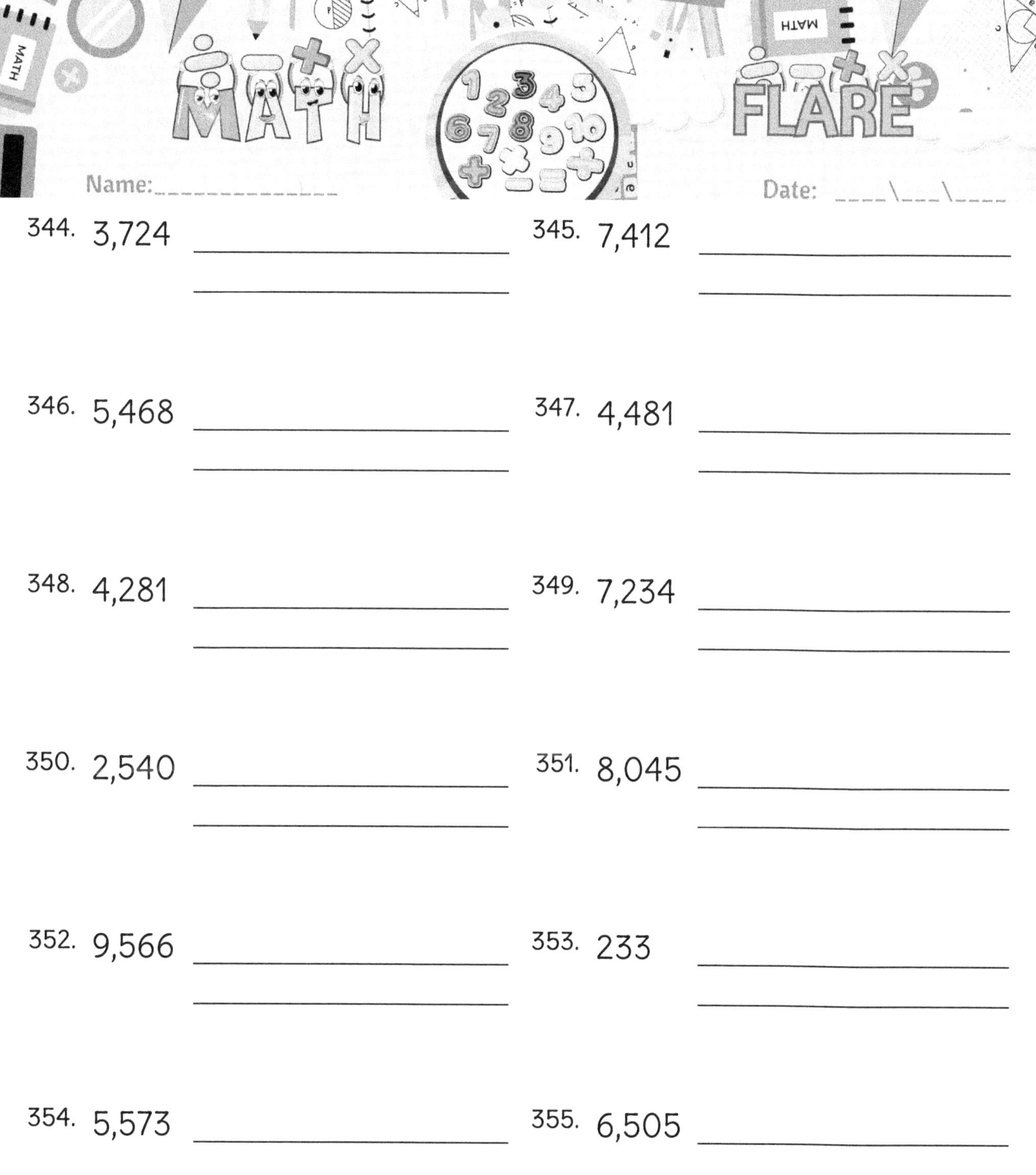

Name:_________________ Date: ____________

344. 3,724 _________________________
____

345. 7,412 _________________________
____

346. 5,468 _________________________
____

347. 4,481 _________________________
____

348. 4,281 _________________________
____

349. 7,234 _________________________
____

350. 2,540 _________________________
____

351. 8,045 _________________________
____

352. 9,566 _________________________
____

353. 233 _________________________
____

354. 5,573 _________________________
____

355. 6,505 _________________________
____

356. 5,344 _________________
____

357. 9,130 _________________
____

358. 1,360 _________________
____

359. 7,034 _________________
____

360. 7,391 _________________
____

361. 1,647 _________________
____

362. 4,984 _________________
____

363. 7,183 _________________
____

364. 2,256 _________________
____

365. 6,308 _________________
____

366. 2,284 _________________
____

367. 9,964 _________________
____

368. 3,938 _______________

369. 9,036 _______________

370. 2,351 _______________

371. 1,613 _______________

372. 2,703 _______________

373. 622 _______________

374. 4,064 _______________

375. 8,925 _______________

376. 9,211 _______________

377. 195 _______________

378. 5,326 _______________

379. 3,425 _______________

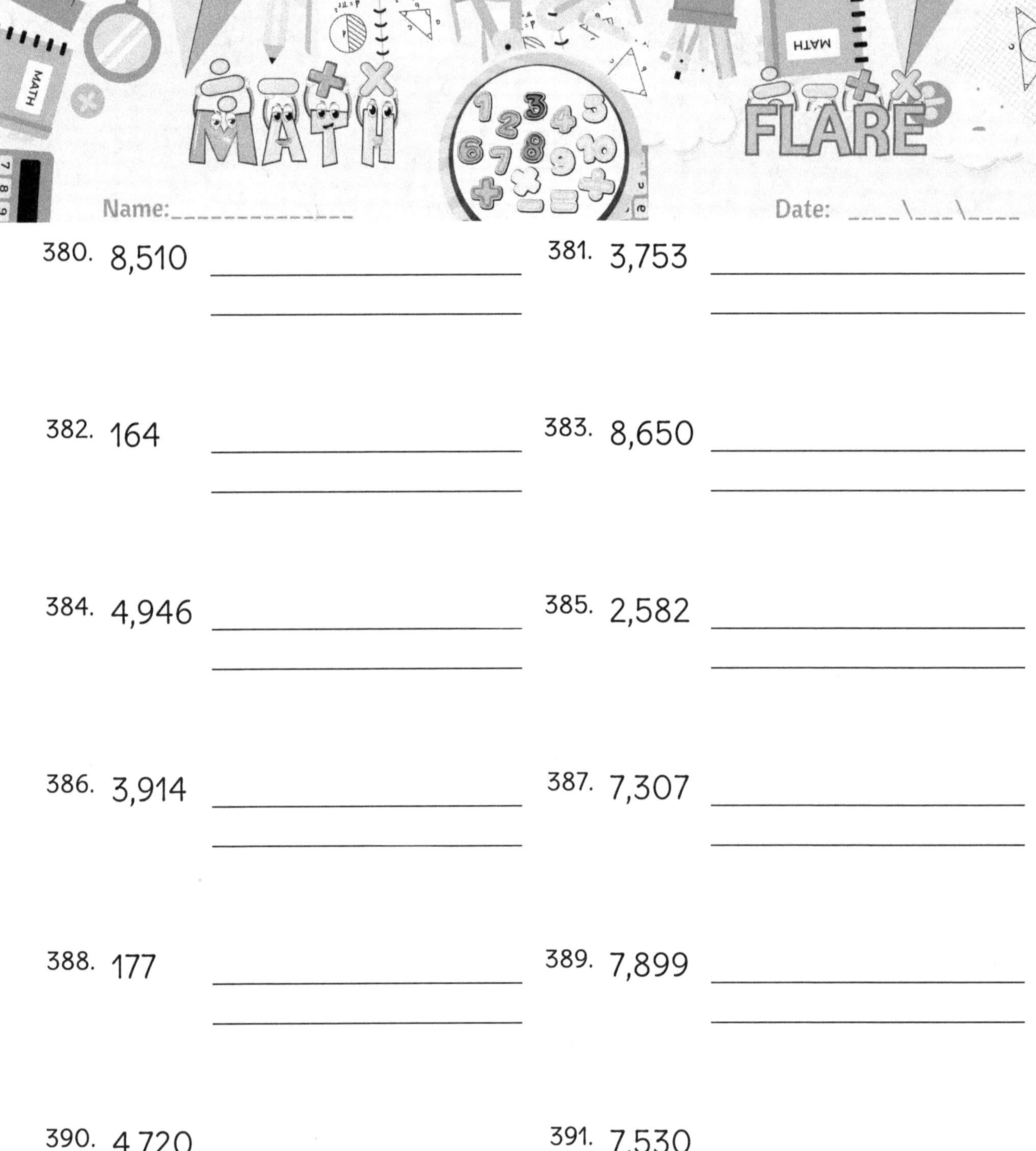

380. 8,510 _______________________

381. 3,753 _______________________

382. 164 _______________________

383. 8,650 _______________________

384. 4,946 _______________________

385. 2,582 _______________________

386. 3,914 _______________________

387. 7,307 _______________________

388. 177 _______________________

389. 7,899 _______________________

390. 4,720 _______________________

391. 7,530 _______________________

392. 8,860 _______________________

393. 9,913 _______________________

394. 1,126 _______________________

395. 1,365 _______________________

396. 5,604 _______________________

397. 4,279 _______________________

398. 6,494 _______________________

399. 7,415 _______________________

400. 5,129 _______________________

401. 5,503 _______________________

402. 544 _______________________

403. 5,244 _______________________

404. 4,884 _______________
____

405. 928 _______________
____

406. 5,343 _______________
____

407. 8,945 _______________
____

408. 6,167 _______________
____

409. 6,647 _______________
____

410. 7,293 _______________
____

411. 5,150 _______________
____

412. 3,804 _______________
____

413. 7,934 _______________
____

414. 8,523 _______________
____

415. 3,639 _______________
____

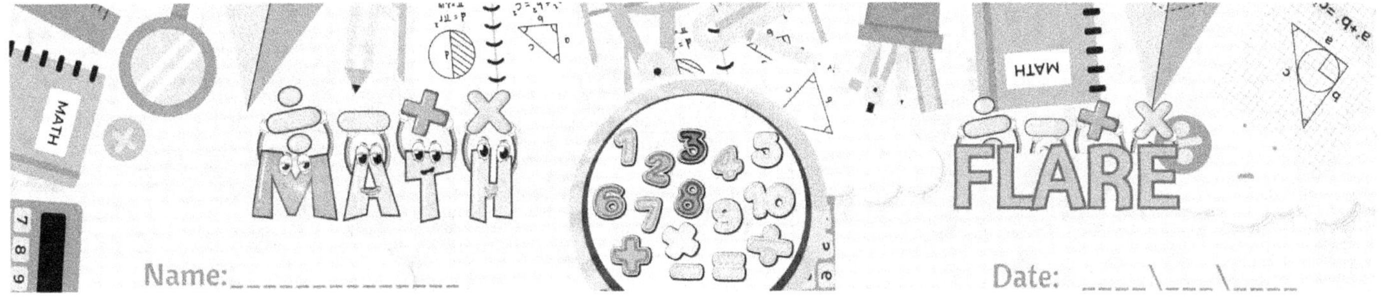

Name:______________   Date: ____________

Place Value: Expanded Notation

Provide the expanded notation for each value.

416. _______________   one thousand four hundred eighty-four

417. _______________   six thousand three hundred thirty-two

418. _______________   two thousand two hundred thirty-eight

419. _______________   nine thousand six hundred seventy-three

420. _______________   two thousand three hundred ninety-four

421. _______________   four thousand nine hundred seventy-six

422. _______________   nine thousand seven hundred eighty-eight

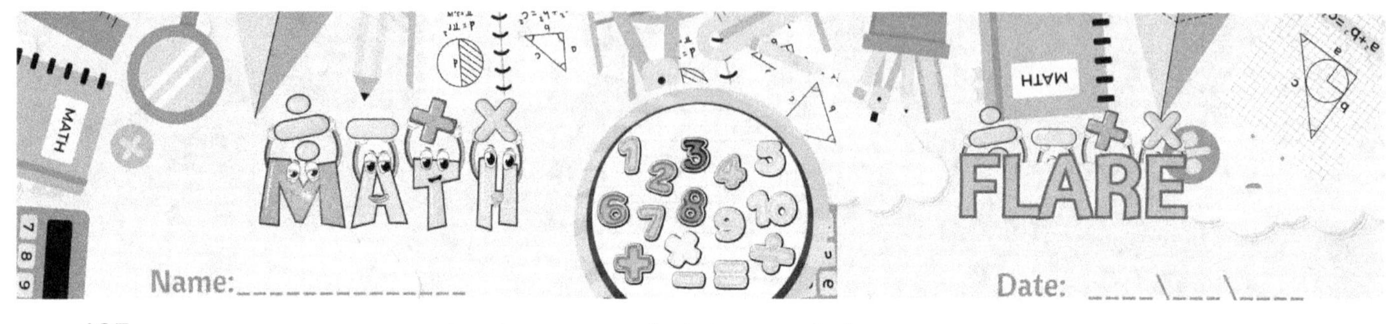

423. ______________ six thousand thirty-eight

424. ______________ four thousand three hundred seventeen

425. ______________ four thousand eight hundred twenty

426. ______________ two thousand seven hundred fifty-two

427. ______________ two thousand seven hundred eighty-eight

428. ______________ nine thousand four hundred ninety-five

429. ______________ two thousand seven hundred one

430. ______________ three thousand three hundred twenty-two

Name:_________________   Date: ___________

431. _______________ four thousand nine hundred thirty-three

432. _______________ three thousand seven hundred

433. _______________ seven thousand nine hundred ten

434. _______________ eight thousand two hundred ninety-five

435. _______________ three thousand eight

436. _______________ three thousand two hundred ten

437. _______________ four thousand nine hundred nineteen

438. _______________ three thousand seven hundred sixty-seven

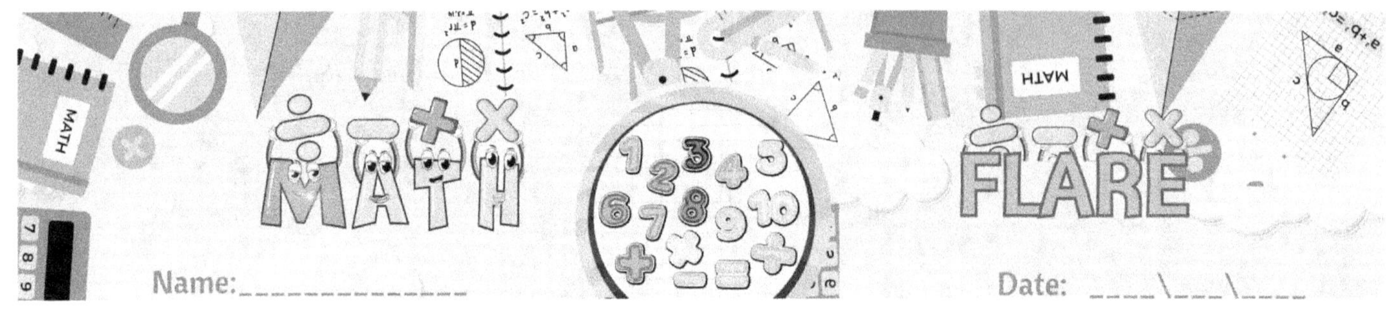

Name:_________________   Date: ____________

439. ______________   four thousand nineteen

440. ______________   seven thousand two hundred thirty-eight

441. ______________   four thousand nine hundred sixty-nine

442. ______________   one thousand one hundred forty-one

443. ______________   three thousand five hundred twenty-nine

444. ______________   six hundred seven

445. ______________   nine thousand five hundred sixty-nine

446. ______________   three thousand seven hundred twenty-seven

447. _______________ nine hundred twenty-seven

448. _______________ one thousand three hundred ninety-two

449. _______________ seven thousand four hundred eighty-five

450. _______________ nine thousand eight hundred seventy-nine

451. _______________ nine thousand two hundred seventy-one

452. _______________ two thousand forty-two

453. _______________ six thousand eight hundred twenty

454. _______________ five thousand twenty-two

455. _______________ one hundred fifty-five

456. _______________ five thousand seven hundred fourteen

457. _______________ four thousand five hundred four

458. _______________ nine hundred twenty-eight

459. _______________ sixty-five

460. _______________ eight thousand one hundred seventy-five

461. _______________ two thousand five hundred fifty-six

462. _______________ nine thousand four hundred forty-nine

MathFlare - Place Value 3rd Grade

44

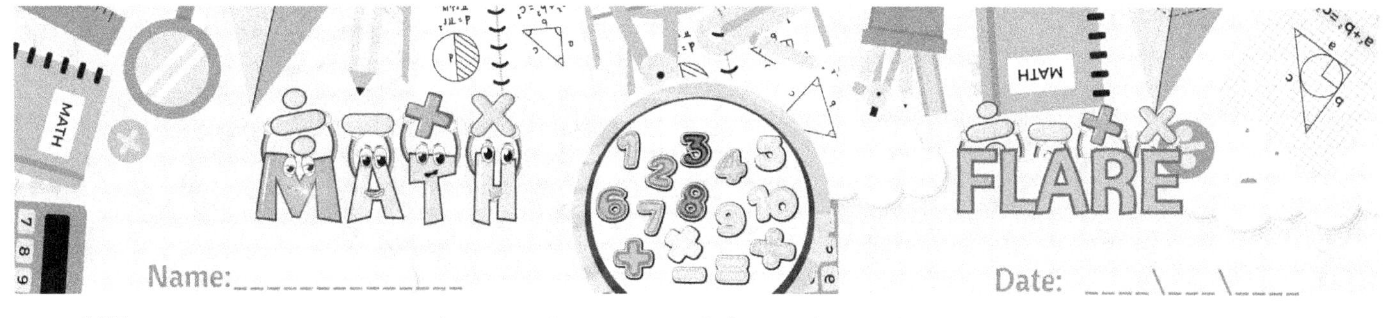

463. _____________ three thousand four hundred sixty-eight

464. _____________ three thousand three hundred twenty-five

465. _____________ two thousand three hundred sixty-one

466. _____________ one thousand four hundred fifty-one

467. _____________ five thousand eight hundred ninety-three

468. _____________ nine thousand six hundred thirty-nine

469. _____________ five thousand five hundred sixteen

470. _____________ four hundred thirty

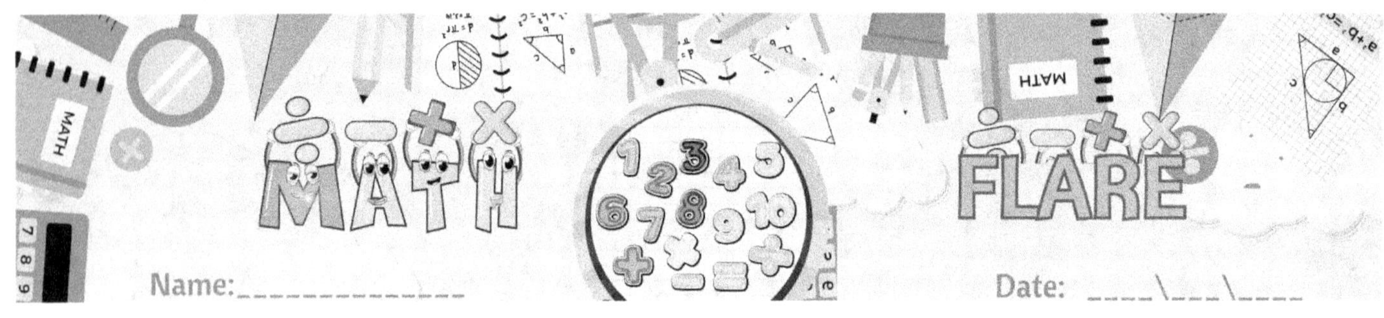

471. _______________ six thousand five hundred sixty-four

472. _______________ two thousand five hundred sixty-six

473. _______________ eight thousand two hundred eighteen

474. _______________ two thousand four hundred thirty-six

475. _______________ seven thousand four hundred twenty-five

476. _______________ three thousand eight hundred thirty-six

477. _______________ six thousand two hundred sixty

478. _______________ five thousand four hundred thirty-three

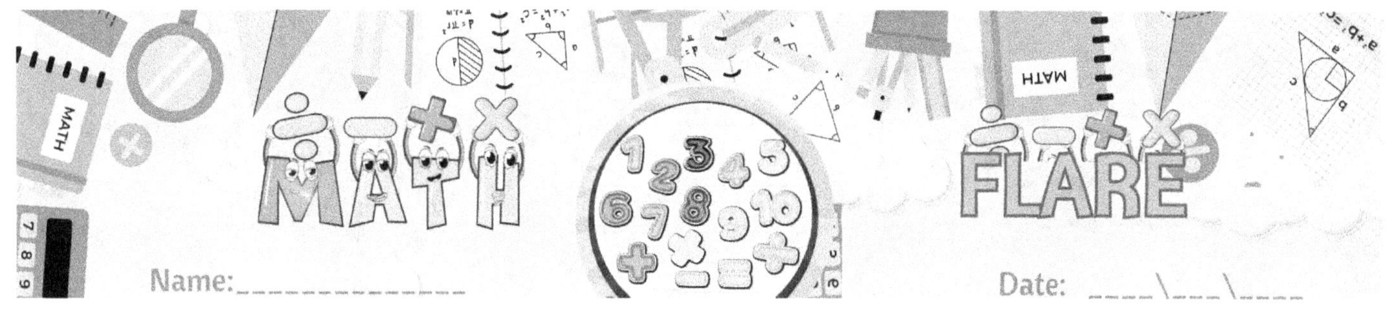

479. __________________ four thousand seven hundred forty-seven

480. __________________ one thousand ninety-four

481. __________________ one thousand eight hundred twenty-six

482. __________________ one thousand three hundred ninety-seven

483. __________________ two thousand eleven

484. __________________ two thousand eight hundred twenty

485. __________________ four thousand fifty

486. __________________ two thousand eight hundred ninety-two

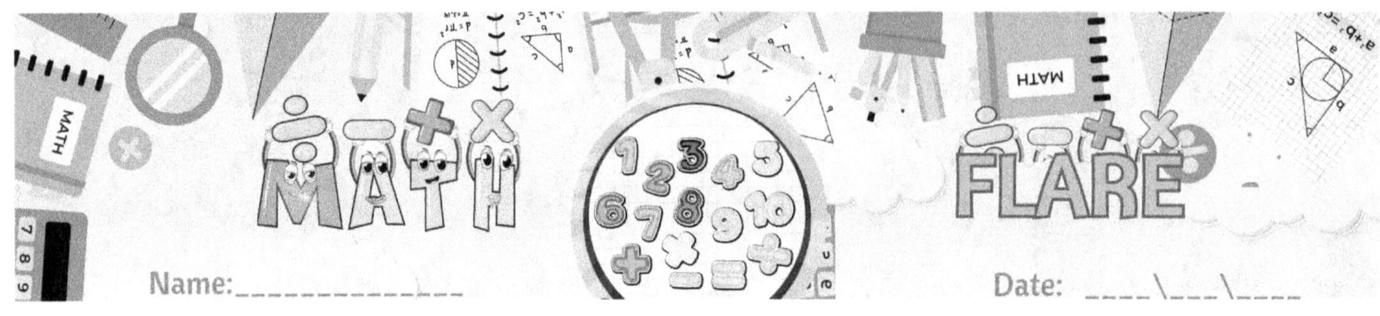

487. _______________ six thousand eight hundred seventy-nine

488. _______________ two thousand eight hundred eighty-nine

489. _______________ eight thousand one hundred forty-one

490. _______________ seven thousand two hundred ninety-three

491. _______________ eight thousand seven hundred five

492. _______________ three thousand nine hundred ninety-two

493. _______________ three thousand seven hundred three

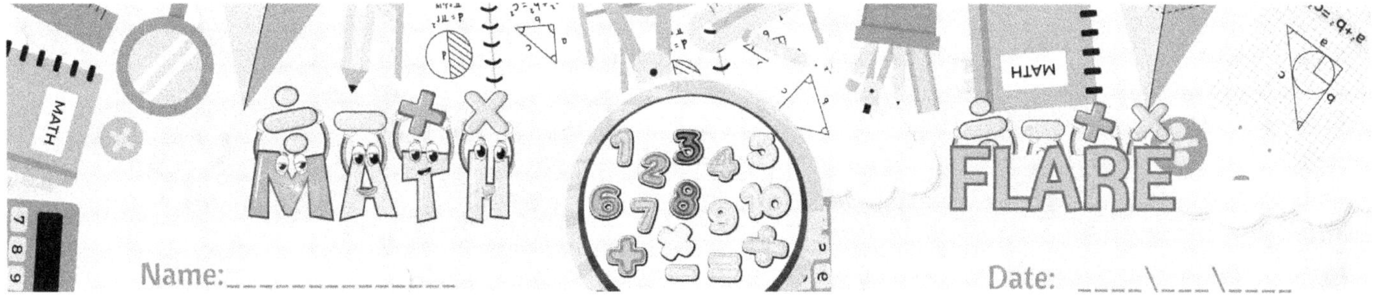

Name:_______________   Date: _____________

Place Value: Expanded Notation

Provide the expanded notation for each value.

494. 871 ___________________   495. 974 ___________________

496. 446 ___________________   497. 169 ___________________

498. 458 ___________________   499. 674 ___________________

500. 731 ___________________   501. 634 ___________________

502. 366 ___________________   503. 712 ___________________

504. 269 __________________
____

505. 361 __________________
____

506. 586 __________________
____

507. 15 __________________
____

508. 39 __________________
____

509. 620 __________________
____

510. 803 __________________
____

511. 970 __________________
____

512. 954 __________________
____

513. 664 __________________
____

514. 491 __________________
____

515. 700 __________________
____

516. 467 ___________________
____

517. 878 ___________________
____

518. 305 ___________________
____

519. 132 ___________________
____

520. 973 ___________________
____

521. 681 ___________________
____

522. 952 ___________________
____

523. 261 ___________________
____

524. 780 ___________________
____

525. 115 ___________________
____

526. 837 ___________________
____

527. 638 ___________________
____

528. 881 __________________________
____

529. 251 __________________________
____

530. 124 __________________________
____

531. 292 __________________________
____

532. 286 __________________________
____

533. 657 __________________________
____

534. 772 __________________________
____

535. 22 __________________________
____

536. 794 __________________________
____

537. 270 __________________________
____

538. 802 __________________________
____

539. 477 __________________________
____

540. 939 _______________________
____

541. 999 _______________________
____

542. 782 _______________________
____

543. 178 _______________________
____

544. 41 _______________________
____

545. 479 _______________________
____

546. 116 _______________________
____

547. 381 _______________________
____

548. 275 _______________________
____

549. 977 _______________________
____

550. 290 _______________________
____

551. 154 _______________________
____

552. 543 _______________

553. 757 _______________

554. 414 _______________

555. 452 _______________

556. 488 _______________

557. 247 _______________

558. 747 _______________

559. 376 _______________

560. 418 _______________

561. 738 _______________

562. 553 _______________

563. 847 _______________

564. 663 _______________________
____

565. 380 _______________________
____

566. 56 _______________________
____

567. 718 _______________________
____

568. 679 _______________________
____

569. 672 _______________________
____

570. 609 _______________________
____

571. 502 _______________________
____

572. 654 _______________________
____

573. 34 _______________________
____

574. 171 _______________________
____

575. 84 _______________________
____

ANSWERS

Page 1:   Place Value

1. 2 ones

2. 6 tens

3. 1 one

4. 9 ones

5. 6 thousands

6. 6 ones

7. 7 ones

8. 7 thousands

9. 3 ones

10. 4 thousands

11. 4 thousands

12. 7 thousands

13. 7 hundreds

14. 4 ones

15. 2 hundreds

16. 4 ones

17. 2 thousands

18. 8 thousands

19. 7 thousands

20. 1 hundred

21. 9 hundreds

22. 2 thousands

23. 0 tens

24. 3 thousands

25. 8 hundreds

26. 7 ones

27. 5 thousands

28. 0 tens

29. 5 hundreds

30. 8 hundreds

31. 6 thousands

32. 8 hundreds

33. 3 tens

34. 0 hundreds

35. 2 thousands

36. 9 thousands

37. 4 thousands

38. 4 tens

39. 9 hundreds

40. 7 hundreds

41. 5 thousands

42. 6 tens

43. 9 tens

44. 3 ones

45. 1 one

46. 0 ones

47. 5 tens

48. 8 ones

49. 5 tens

50. 6 tens

51. 2 hundreds

52. 0 tens

53. 0 ones

54. 8 thousands

55. 2 thousands

56. 0 hundreds

57. 9 hundreds

58. 7 ones 59. 3 thousands 60. 9 thousands

61. 9 hundreds 62. 7 ones 63. 2 ones

64. 3 thousands 65. 8 thousands 66. 1 ten

67. 5 thousands 68. 7 tens 69. 7 tens

70. 6 ones 71. 4 tens 72. 4 hundreds

73. 8 thousands 74. 4 thousands 75. 0 tens

76. 7 hundreds 77. 0 hundreds 78. 7 tens

79. 5 hundreds 80. 4 tens 81. 8 thousands

82. 1 one 83. 1 hundred 84. 9 thousands

85. 0 tens 86. 6 thousands 87. 0 hundreds

88. 0 hundreds 89. 5 tens 90. 7 tens

91. 6 thousands 92. 8 ones 93. 3 tens

94. 3 tens

Page 7: Place Value: Expanded Notation

95. 9,365 96. 6,067 97. 3,631 98. 7,762 99. 2,143

100. 3,446 101. 4,872 102. 5,962 103. 4,426 104. 7,170

105. 6,490 106. 9,602 107. 6,640 108. 3,722 109. 2,763

110. 373 111. 7,355 112. 9,769 113. 66 114. 4,717

115. 3,366 116. 580 117. 6,220 118. 5,506 119. 9,753

120. 9,558 121. 4,429 122. 6,347 123. 2,310 124. 8,526

125. 9,267 126. 7,470 127. 3,297 128. 7,186 129. 9,689

130. 7,386   131. 4,108   132. 2,888   133. 4,029   134. 829

135. 6,912   136. 5,781   137. 4,195   138. 2,949   139. 6,237

140. 3,899   141. 9,928   142. 1,881   143. 2,495   144. 8,633

145. 4,754   146. 1,561   147. 8,839   148. 4,765   149. 5,237

150. 8,785   151. 9,846   152. 8,124   153. 8,008   154. 2,584

155. 9,016   156. 8,523   157. 3,653   158. 5,898   159. 7,901

160. 9,018   161. 6,305   162. 9,453   163. 4,031   164. 5,376

165. 6,264   166. 4,467   167. 5,741   168. 9,236   169. 7,805

170. 7,584   171. 6,384   172. 3,272   173. 9,268

Page 17: Place Value: Expanded Notation

174. 9 thousands + 9 hundreds + 1 ten + 8 ones

175. 9 thousands + 8 hundreds + 2 tens + 4 ones

176. 4 thousands + 3 hundreds + 8 tens + 4 ones

177. 6 thousands + 8 hundreds + 2 tens + 4 ones

178. 9 thousands + 7 hundreds + 4 tens + 9 ones

179. 4 thousands + 8 hundreds + 2 tens + 2 ones

180. 6 thousands + 4 hundreds + 2 tens + 6 ones

181. 9 thousands + 8 hundreds + 7 tens + 7 ones

182. 5 thousands + 4 tens

183. 2 hundreds + 8 tens + 1 one

184. 8 thousands + 9 hundreds + 4 tens + 6 ones

185. 4 thousands + 6 hundreds + 4 tens + 7 ones

186. 6 thousands + 7 hundreds + 5 tens + 3 ones

187. 2 thousands + 1 hundred + 9 tens + 1 one

188. 3 thousands + 2 hundreds + 7 ones

189. 1 thousand + 7 hundreds + 9 tens + 3 ones

190. 7 thousands + 6 hundreds + 3 tens + 4 ones

191. 8 thousands + 7 hundreds + 3 tens + 9 ones

192. 3 thousands + 3 hundreds + 9 tens + 1 one

193. 7 thousands + 8 tens + 4 ones

194. 1 thousand + 7 hundreds + 8 tens + 5 ones

195. 5 thousands + 2 hundreds + 9 tens + 6 ones

196. 4 thousands + 2 tens + 5 ones

197. 1 thousand + 6 hundreds + 8 tens + 1 one

198. 8 thousands + 6 hundreds + 7 ones

199. 9 hundreds + 6 tens + 4 ones

200. 1 thousand + 4 hundreds + 5 tens + 4 ones

201. 8 thousands + 6 hundreds + 4 tens + 9 ones

202. 9 thousands + 6 hundreds + 6 tens + 3 ones

203. 8 thousands + 1 hundred + 5 tens + 3 ones

204. 6 thousands + 1 hundred + 6 ones

205. 5 thousands + 8 hundreds + 1 ten + 8 ones

206. 4 thousands + 6 hundreds + 1 ten

207. 1 thousand + 5 hundreds + 9 tens + 3 ones

208. 1 thousand + 9 hundreds + 2 tens + 3 ones

209. 9 thousands + 6 tens + 7 ones

210. 8 thousands + 1 ten + 3 ones

211. 8 thousands + 1 hundred + 5 tens + 4 ones

212. 1 thousand + 8 hundreds + 3 tens + 4 ones

213. 6 hundreds + 2 tens + 6 ones

214. 1 thousand + 1 hundred + 8 tens + 5 ones

215. 1 thousand + 9 hundreds + 1 ten + 3 ones

216. 5 thousands + 4 hundreds + 4 tens + 5 ones

217. 9 thousands + 1 hundred + 7 tens + 4 ones

218. 6 thousands + 9 hundreds + 5 ones

219. 3 thousands + 2 hundreds + 9 tens + 3 ones

220. 7 thousands + 7 hundreds + 5 tens + 4 ones

221. 9 thousands + 9 hundreds + 7 tens + 6 ones

222. 7 thousands + 9 hundreds + 2 ones

223. 8 thousands + 6 hundreds + 4 tens + 2 ones

224. 6 thousands + 6 hundreds + 2 tens + 3 ones

225. 4 thousands + 9 tens

226. 4 thousands + 6 hundreds + 3 tens + 1 one

227. 6 thousands + 7 hundreds + 2 tens

228. 4 thousands + 6 hundreds + 2 tens + 3 ones

229. 5 thousands + 8 hundreds

230. 2 thousands + 7 hundreds + 4 ones

231. 8 thousands + 2 hundreds + 1 ten + 5 ones

232. 8 thousands + 7 hundreds + 8 tens + 6 ones

233. 3 thousands + 3 hundreds + 6 tens + 9 ones

234. 7 thousands + 7 hundreds + 7 tens + 6 ones

235. 2 hundreds + 1 ten + 5 ones

236. 6 thousands + 8 hundreds + 8 tens + 6 ones

237. 4 thousands + 1 hundred + 7 tens + 4 ones

238. 3 thousands + 1 hundred + 3 tens

239. 3 tens + 8 ones

240. 5 thousands + 1 hundred + 6 tens + 1 one

241. 2 hundreds + 6 tens + 8 ones

242. 4 thousands + 1 hundred + 4 tens

243. 3 thousands + 7 hundreds + 7 tens + 9 ones

244. 9 thousands + 4 hundreds + 7 tens + 9 ones

245. 6 thousands + 9 hundreds + 6 ones

246. 2 thousands + 7 hundreds + 6 tens + 6 ones

247. 5 thousands + 9 hundreds

248. 9 thousands + 8 hundreds + 7 tens + 1 one

249. 9 thousands + 8 hundreds + 5 tens

250. 4 thousands + 8 hundreds + 5 tens

251. 4 thousands + 7 hundreds + 7 tens + 5 ones

Page 25: Place Value: Expanded Notation

252. 6,681	253. 3,916	254. 3,002	255. 6,527	256. 1,207
257. 1,974	258. 4,669	259. 6,552	260. 9,926	261. 3,454
262. 3,853	263. 4,251	264. 7,611	265. 3,280	266. 6,175
267. 972	268. 6,806	269. 577	270. 2,562	271. 8,071
272. 5,162	273. 1,057	274. 7,825	275. 2,133	276. 1,859
277. 8,323	278. 2,185	279. 4,846	280. 838	281. 1,585
282. 4,353	283. 4,841	284. 2,418	285. 7,961	286. 4,142
287. 9,100	288. 1,458	289. 6,132	290. 1,633	291. 3,512
292. 7,235	293. 1,184	294. 2,824	295. 3,383	296. 6,246
297. 4,373	298. 7,696	299. 8,704	300. 7,306	301. 5,088
302. 7,179	303. 4,288	304. 8,180	305. 2,197	306. 1,014
307. 5,625	308. 6,090	309. 870	310. 2,883	311. 9,787
312. 9,822	313. 5,715	314. 8,342	315. 9,101	316. 9,011
317. 1,834	318. 9,650	319. 9,137	320. 7,074	321. 9,513
322. 675	323. 8,943	324. 9,049	325. 3,979	326. 8,233
327. 4,444	328. 5,886	329. 7,485	330. 628	331. 3,481

332. 7,539   333. 5,749

Page 32:   Place Value: Expanded Notation

334. 4,000 + 400 + 5

335. 60 + 5

336. 6,000 + 600 + 60 + 1

337. 200 + 20 + 2

338. 6,000 + 900 + 40 + 8

339. 8,000 + 500 + 10 + 6

340. 3,000 + 10 + 1

341. 500 + 80 + 9

342. 1,000 + 400 + 60 + 3

343. 8,000 + 700 + 40 + 9

344. 3,000 + 700 + 20 + 4

345. 7,000 + 400 + 10 + 2

346. 5,000 + 400 + 60 + 8

347. 4,000 + 400 + 80 + 1

348. 4,000 + 200 + 80 + 1

349. 7,000 + 200 + 30 + 4

350. 2,000 + 500 + 40

351. 8,000 + 40 + 5

352. 9,000 + 500 + 60 + 6

353. 200 + 30 + 3

354. 5,000 + 500 + 70 + 3

355. 6,000 + 500 + 5

356. 5,000 + 300 + 40 + 4

357. 9,000 + 100 + 30

358. 1,000 + 300 + 60

359. 7,000 + 30 + 4

360. 7,000 + 300 + 90 + 1

361. 1,000 + 600 + 40 + 7

362. 4,000 + 900 + 80 + 4

363. 7,000 + 100 + 80 + 3

364. 2,000 + 200 + 50 + 6

365. 6,000 + 300 + 8

366. 2,000 + 200 + 80 + 4

367. 9,000 + 900 + 60 + 4

368. 3,000 + 900 + 30 + 8

369. 9,000 + 30 + 6

370. 2,000 + 300 + 50 + 1

371. 1,000 + 600 + 10 + 3

372. 2,000 + 700 + 3

373. 600 + 20 + 2

374. 4,000 + 60 + 4

375. 8,000 + 900 + 20 + 5

376. 9,000 + 200 + 10 + 1

377. 100 + 90 + 5

378. 5,000 + 300 + 20 + 6

379. 3,000 + 400 + 20 + 5

380. 8,000 + 500 + 10

381. 3,000 + 700 + 50 + 3

382. 100 + 60 + 4

383. 8,000 + 600 + 50

384. 4,000 + 900 + 40 + 6

385. 2,000 + 500 + 80 + 2

386. 3,000 + 900 + 10 + 4

387. 7,000 + 300 + 7

388. 100 + 70 + 7

389. 7,000 + 800 + 90 + 9

390. 4,000 + 700 + 20

391. 7,000 + 500 + 30

392. 8,000 + 800 + 60

393. 9,000 + 900 + 10 + 3

394. 1,000 + 100 + 20 + 6

395. 1,000 + 300 + 60 + 5

396. 5,000 + 600 + 4

397. 4,000 + 200 + 70 + 9

398. 6,000 + 400 + 90 + 4

399. 7,000 + 400 + 10 + 5

400. 5,000 + 100 + 20 + 9

401. 5,000 + 500 + 3

402. 500 + 40 + 4

403. 5,000 + 200 + 40 + 4

404. 4,000 + 800 + 80 + 4

405. 900 + 20 + 8

406. 5,000 + 300 + 40 + 3

407. 8,000 + 900 + 40 + 5

408. 6,000 + 100 + 60 + 7

409. 6,000 + 600 + 40 + 7

410. 7,000 + 200 + 90 + 3

411. 5,000 + 100 + 50

412. 3,000 + 800 + 4

413. 7,000 + 900 + 30 + 4

414. 8,000 + 500 + 20 + 3   415. 3,000 + 600 + 30 + 9

Page 39: Place Value: Expanded Notation

416. 1,484	417. 6,332	418. 2,238	419. 9,673	420. 2,394
421. 4,976	422. 9,788	423. 6,038	424. 4,317	425. 4,820
426. 2,752	427. 2,788	428. 9,495	429. 2,701	430. 3,322
431. 4,933	432. 3,700	433. 7,910	434. 8,295	435. 3,008
436. 3,210	437. 4,919	438. 3,767	439. 4,019	440. 7,238
441. 4,969	442. 1,141	443. 3,529	444. 607	445. 9,569
446. 3,727	447. 927	448. 1,392	449. 7,485	450. 9,879
451. 9,271	452. 2,042	453. 6,820	454. 5,022	455. 155
456. 5,714	457. 4,504	458. 928	459. 65	460. 8,175
461. 2,556	462. 9,449	463. 3,468	464. 3,325	465. 2,361
466. 1,451	467. 5,893	468. 9,639	469. 5,516	470. 430
471. 6,564	472. 2,566	473. 8,218	474. 2,436	475. 7,425
476. 3,836	477. 6,260	478. 5,433	479. 4,747	480. 1,094
481. 1,826	482. 1,397	483. 2,011	484. 2,820	485. 4,050
486. 2,892	487. 6,879	488. 2,889	489. 8,141	490. 7,293
491. 8,705	492. 3,992	493. 3,703		

Page 49: Place Value: Expanded Notation

494. eight hundred seventy-one   495. nine hundred seventy-four

496. four hundred forty-six   497. one hundred sixty-nine

498. four hundred fifty-eight

499. six hundred seventy-four

500. seven hundred thirty-one

501. six hundred thirty-four

502. three hundred sixty-six

503. seven hundred twelve

504. two hundred sixty-nine

505. three hundred sixty-one

506. five hundred eighty-six

507. fifteen

508. thirty-nine

509. six hundred twenty

510. eight hundred three

511. nine hundred seventy

512. nine hundred fifty-four

513. six hundred sixty-four

514. four hundred ninety-one

515. seven hundred

516. four hundred sixty-seven

517. eight hundred seventy-eight

518. three hundred five

519. one hundred thirty-two

520. nine hundred seventy-three

521. six hundred eighty-one

522. nine hundred fifty-two

523. two hundred sixty-one

524. seven hundred eighty

525. one hundred fifteen

526. eight hundred thirty-seven

527. six hundred thirty-eight

528. eight hundred eighty-one

529. two hundred fifty-one

530. one hundred twenty-four

531. two hundred ninety-two

532. two hundred eighty-six

533. six hundred fifty-seven

534. seven hundred seventy-two

535. twenty-two

536. seven hundred ninety-four

537. two hundred seventy

538. eight hundred two

539. four hundred seventy-seven

540. nine hundred thirty-nine

541. nine hundred ninety-nine

542. seven hundred eighty-two

543. one hundred seventy-eight

544. forty-one

545. four hundred seventy-nine

546. one hundred sixteen

547. three hundred eighty-one

548. two hundred seventy-five

549. nine hundred seventy-seven

550. two hundred ninety

551. one hundred fifty-four

552. five hundred forty-three

553. seven hundred fifty-seven

554. four hundred fourteen

555. four hundred fifty-two

556. four hundred eighty-eight

557. two hundred forty-seven

558. seven hundred forty-seven

559. three hundred seventy-six

560. four hundred eighteen

561. seven hundred thirty-eight

562. five hundred fifty-three

563. eight hundred forty-seven

564. six hundred sixty-three

565. three hundred eighty

566. fifty-six

567. seven hundred eighteen

568. six hundred seventy-nine

569. six hundred seventy-two

570. six hundred nine

571. five hundred two

572. six hundred fifty-four

573. thirty-four

574. one hundred seventy-one

575. eighty-four